Look-alike Animals

# IS IT A FROG OR A TOAD?

Susan B. Katz

raintree
a Capstone company — publishers for children

Raintree is an imprint of Capstone Global Library Limited, a company incorporated in England and Wales having its registered office at 264 Banbury Road, Oxford, OX2 7DY – Registered company number: 6695582

www.raintree.co.uk
myorders@raintree.co.uk

Edited by Christianne Jones
Designed by Elyse White
Original illustrations © Capstone Global Library Limited 2022
Picture research by Svetlana Zhurkin
Production by Laura Manthe
Originated by Capstone Global Library Ltd
Printed and bound in India

978 1 3982 2563 3 (hardback)
978 1 3982 2564 0 (paperback)

**British Library Cataloguing in Publication Data**
A full catalogue record for this book is available from the British Library.

**Acknowledgements**
We would like to thank the following for permission to reproduce photographs: Dreamstime: Lucian Milasan, 10; Shutterstock: AcidRoot, 14, Angel DiBilio, 12, Anna_Kova (design element), cover (middle) and throughout, Bildagentur Zoonar GmbH, 6, Boxyray, 8, Brian Lasenby, 27, Cathy Keifer, 16, David Havel, 9, Dinda Yulianto, cover (top), Dirk Ercken, 28, Eriks Roze, 11, FJAH, 17, Guide Pst, 5, Huaykwang, 21, IrinaK, 7, Jan Gottwald, 25, Karel Bock, 31, LegART, 3, Liz Miller, 29, Louis.Roth, 15 (bottom), meunierd, 30, Michael Benard, 18, 19, 20, 22, Milan Zygmunt, 24, motorolka, cover (bottom), Muhammad Naaim, 13, photowind, 15 (top), Pyshnyy Maxim Vjacheslavovich, 4, Rainer Fuhrmann, 26, scubaluna, 23.

Every effort has been made to contact copyright holders of material reproduced in this book. Any omissions will be rectified in subsequent printings if notice is given to the publisher.

All the internet addresses (URLs) given in this book were valid at the time of going to press. However, due to the dynamic nature of the internet, some addresses may have changed, or sites may have changed or ceased to exist since publication. While the author and publisher regret any inconvenience this may cause readers, no responsibility for any such changes can be accepted by either the author or the publisher.

What is that creature jumping along the road? Is it a **frog** or a **toad?** Frogs and toads have many **similarities** and **differences.** Toads are actually a certain type of frog.

Let's **leap in** and learn **more!**

Is that a rock in your garden? **No!** It's a toad! Toads can stay on **dry land** longer than frogs.

toad

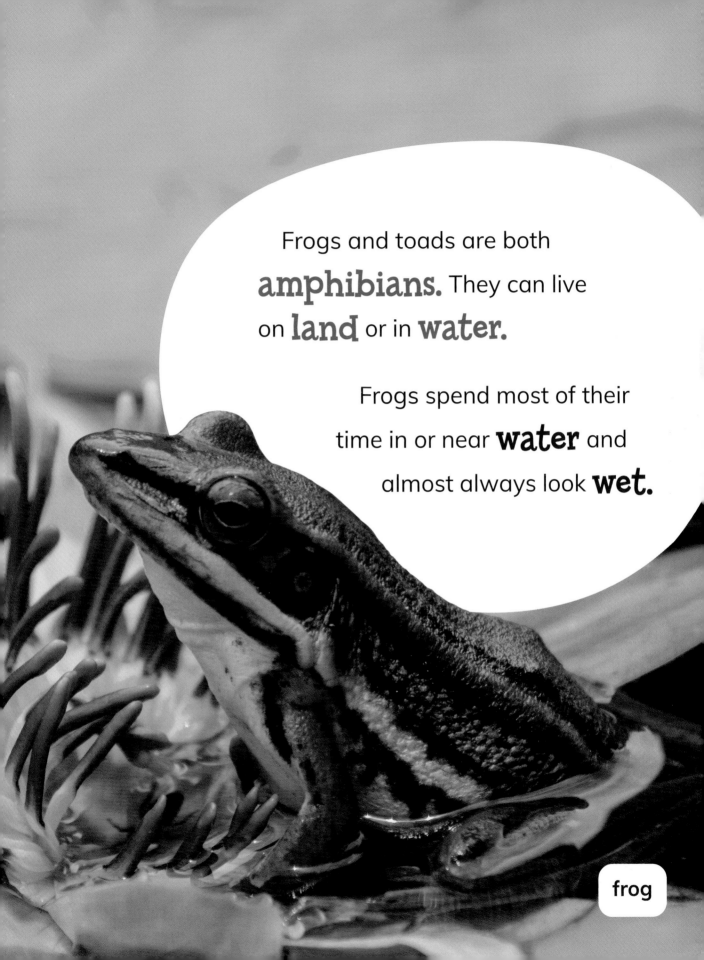

Frogs and toads are both **amphibians.** They can live on **land** or in **water.**

Frogs spend most of their time in or near **water** and almost always look **wet.**

frog

Toads stay in **wet, open habitats** like grasslands, fields and gardens.

toad

Frogs like being near

## fresh water

that doesn't move fast, such as lakes, ponds and marshes. They can't survive in **salt water** like oceans and seas.

frog

Have you heard that you can get warts from touching a toad? It's not true! But a toad's skin is **lumpy** and **bumpy** and is usually **brown** or **green.**

toad

frog

Most frogs have **slimy, wet, smooth skin.**

They can be **green** or **brown.**

They also come in many bright colours like **yellow, red** and **blue.**

frog

Most frogs have **long hind legs** that help them **climb, leap, hop** and **swim.** They can **jump very high.**

A frog's legs are longer than its head and body.

Toads have **shorter legs** that look like **stumps.** They **crawl** or **walk** and **hop,** but they **rarely leap.**

toad

# It's time to be
## nosy!

Frogs have thin faces with **pointed noses.** Toads have rounder faces with **wider noses**.

frog

Frogs often have **high, big, bulging eyes.** They can see all around them without even turning their heads!

Toads have poison glands behind their **football-shaped eyes,** so they **don't see** so well.

toad

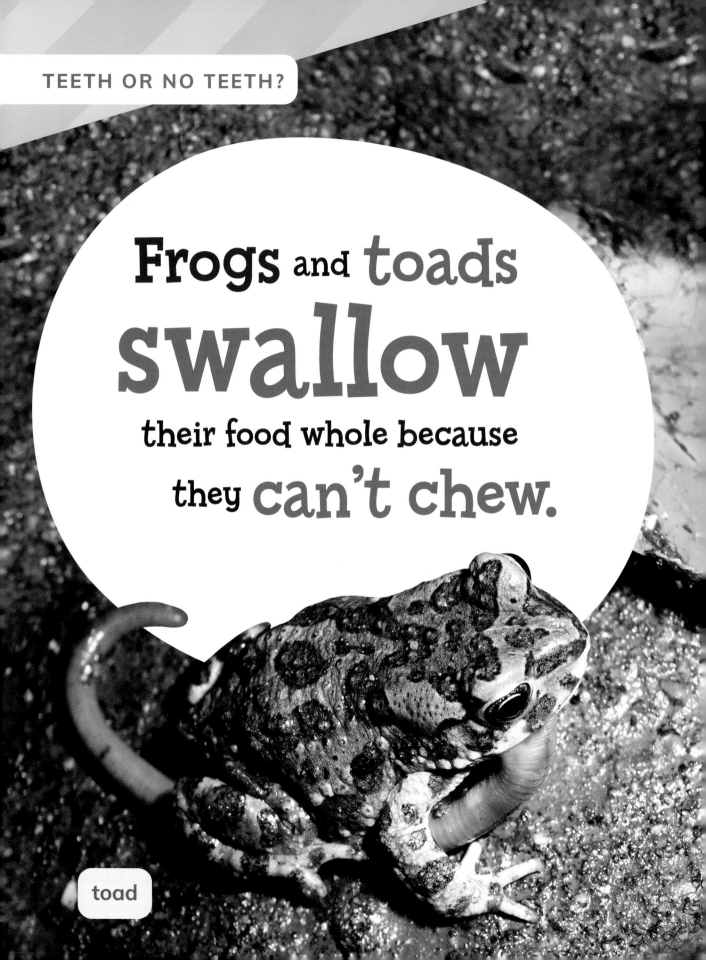

Frogs and toads swallow their food whole because they can't chew.

toad

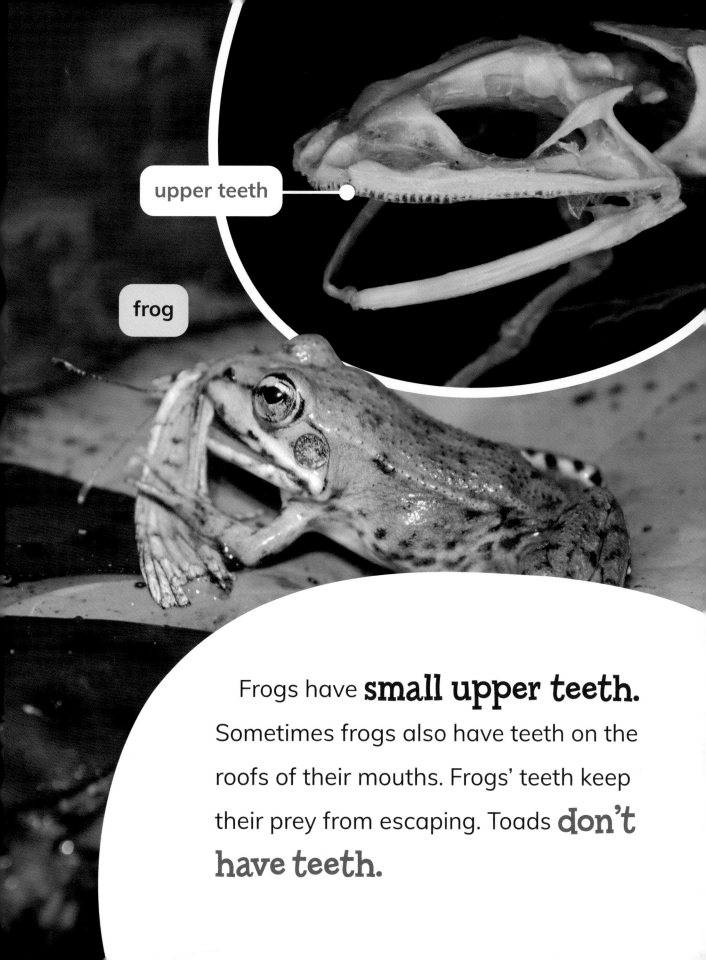

upper teeth

frog

Frogs have **small upper teeth.** Sometimes frogs also have teeth on the roofs of their mouths. Frogs' teeth keep their prey from escaping. Toads **don't have teeth.**

# Dinner
## is served!

Frogs have **short** but **fast** and **strong tongues.** A frog grabs its prey by quickly leaping and sticking out its tongue, **wrapping** it around an insect.

frog

Toads' **tongues** are usually **longer.** When a toad sees a snack, it crawls close enough to grab it with a **quick flick** of its **long** tongue.

toad

# Frogs and toads are carnivores, meaning they eat meat.

Most frogs **eat insects.** Some bigger frogs eat worms, small snakes, mice, baby turtles or smaller frogs!

frog

toad

Toads **eat anything** they can fit in their mouths, including flies, spiders, slugs, snails, worms and grasshoppers.

**Frogs** and **toads** can creek, croak, whistle, ribbit, grunt and **more!**

frog

Every type of frog and toad makes its own **unique sound** for different reasons. Usually only **male** frogs and toads **croak.** The loud croaking **attracts females.**

toad

frog eggs

# Frogs and toads both lay eggs.

They must be in or near water to lay and hatch their eggs.

toad eggs

Frogs lay their **eggs** in **gooey clumps** that look like lots of clear grapes with black dots. Toad eggs **float** in **long strands.**

When frogs and toads are babies, or **tadpoles,** they have tails. They also have **gills** like fish and **breathe underwater.**

frog tadpole

toad tadpole

Frog tadpoles are **skinny.** They are **greenish grey** or **brownish** in colour and are covered in flecks. Toad tadpoles are **chunkier** and **black.**

A snake eating a toad

Toad **skin** tastes and smells **bitter.** It burns a **predator's eyes** and **nostrils.** Grass snakes, otters and hedgehogs eat toads.

A bird eating a frog

**Many animals eat frogs,** including herons, grass snakes and otters.

**Poison arrow frogs,** also known as poison dart frogs, live in the **rainforests** of Central and South America. Their **bright colour** lets predators know that they are **deadly.**

poison arrow frog

cane toad

Toads can be **toxic** too. The **cane toad** is the **largest** known toad. It is very **poisonous** and makes a **milky, white toxin** on its back.

Goliath frog

Frogs and toads live in

# every climate

and on **every continent**

of the world except Antarctica.

The **Goliath frog** is the **biggest** frog and is found in **Africa**. It **weighs** as much as a **newborn baby**.

The world's **smallest frogs** live mostly in the rainforests. They are **smaller** than your **thumbnail!**

frog

# IS IT A FROG OR A TOAD?

1. Its smooth, wet skin shines as it swims. Is it a frog or a toad?

2. A plump, brown animal with bumpy skin sits in the garden. Is it a frog or a toad?

3. This animal can see around it without turning its head. Is it a frog or a toad?

4. This amphibian has a longer tongue. Is it a frog or a toad?

5. This animal has a rounder face and wider nose. Is it a frog or a toad?

Answer key: 1. frog 2. toad 3. frog 4. toad 5. toad